What's Living Inside Your Body?

Andrew Solway

Heinemann Library
Chicago, Illinois

Customer Service 888-454-2279
Visit our website at www.heinemannlibrary.com

Designed by David Poole and Paul Myerscough
Illustrations by Geoff Ward
Originated by Dot Gradations
Printed and bound in China by South China Printing Company

08 07 06
10 9 8 7 6 5 4 3 2

Library of Congress Cataloging-in-Publication Data
Solway, Andrew.
  What's living inside your body? : Andrew Solway.
     v. cm. -- (Hidden life)
Includes bibliographical references and index.
Contents: Take a closer look -- Microbes in the mouth -- Bacteria in the gut -- Trouble in the gut -- Worms -- Tapeworms -- Microbes in the nose and throat -- Sore throats, cold, and flu -- Microbes in the lungs -- Microbes in the blood -- Diseases from blood-suckers.
  ISBN 1-4034-4847-7 (HC library binding) -- ISBN 1-4034-5486-8 (PB)
  1. Body, Human--Microbiology--Juvenile literature. [1. Body, Human. 2. Microorganisms.] I. Title. II. Series.
  QR171.A1S648 2004
  612--dc22

2003018003

Acknowledgments
The author and publishers are grateful to the following for permission to reproduce copyright material: Science Photo Library p. 4 (Simon Fraser), p. 5 (R. Maisonneuve, Publiphoto Diffusion), pp. 6t, 9b, 15 (CNRI), p. 6b (Dr Tony Brain), p. 7 (Volker Steger, p. 8 (BSIP, Vero/Carlo), p. 9t (Prof. P. Motta), pp. 10L, 22r (Dr Linda Stannard, UCT), pp. 12, 19 (Dr P. Marazzi), p. 13 (David Scharf), pp. 14, 17, 23, 26t, 27t, 27b (Eye of Science), 16 (Juergen Berger, Max Planck Institute), pp. 16t, 17t, 18t (Alfred Pasieka), p. 18b, (Susumu Nishinaga), p. 21t (CAMR/Barry Dowsett), p. 21b (Chris Priest and Mark Clarke), p. 24 (Jack K. Clark), p. 25 (Dr Gary Gaugler), p. 26b (Michael Abbey); Science Photo Library pp. 10r, 11, 20; Trevor Clifford p. 22L.

Cover photograph of a hookworm, reproduced with permission of Science Photo Library/David Scharf.

Our thanks to Dr. Philip Parrillo, entomologist at the Field Museum in Chicago, for his comments in the preparation of this book.

Every effort has been made to contact copyright holders of any material reproduced in this book. Any omissions will be rectified in subsequent printings if notice is given to the publishers.

Some words are shown in bold, **like this.** You can find out what they mean by looking in the glossary.

Contents

Many of the photos in this book were taken using a microscope.
In the captions you may see a number that tells you how
much they have been enlarged. For example, a photo marked
"(x200)" is about 200 times bigger than in real life.

Taking a Closer Look

We all know that germs can cause disease if they get inside our bodies. We wash our hands before we eat so that we do not get germs on our food. Also, we clean cuts and scrapes carefully to stop them from getting infected with germs. Germs are **microbes**—tiny living things too small to see without a microscope.

Microbes can cause disease, but even healthy people have lots of microbes inside their body. More microbes live inside you than there are humans on the planet. Most cause no harm, and some are very helpful. Nearly all these microbes live in your nose, mouth, and **gut.** But sometimes they get into the blood or other parts of the body and make you ill.

Today, doctors can use modern medical machines to look at the organs and bones inside the body. But these machines do not show the hidden life inside us.

Unwelcome visitors

Bigger animals, **parasites** such as **tapeworms** and **hookworms,** can also live inside us. However, these parasites do not usually infect people in **developed countries.** The idea of having worms living inside you is pretty horrible, but some types of worms can actually live inside you without making you ill.

Smaller residents

Microbes are much more common in the body than larger creatures. Most of the microbes in our bodies are **bacteria.** Different kinds of bacteria can be as different from one another as people are from insects. Some kinds of bacteria make their home in our gut, and they live there happily without harming us. But if other types get inside us, they can cause disease. Luckily, our bodies have many defense systems against disease-causing microbes.

Electron microscopes are expensive and difficult to use, but they can magnify objects much more than a light microscope can.

MICROSCOPES

We know so much about the hidden life all around us because scientists have used microscopes to study these things. A light microscope, the type of microscope you may have used yourself at home or at school, can magnify objects up to about 1,800 times. But to look at really tiny things such as bacteria, scientists use powerful electron microscopes, which can magnify objects 500,000 times.

Microbes in the Mouth

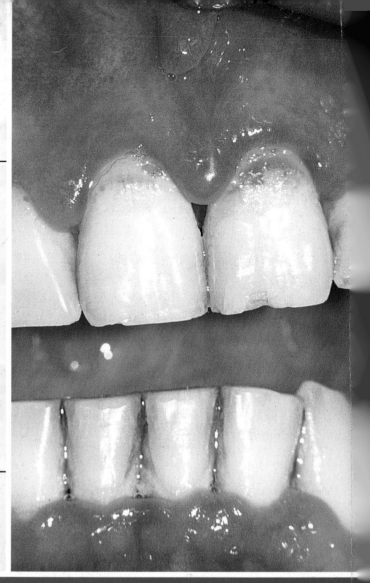

Every time you eat or put something into your mouth, you put **microbes** in there, too. You begin doing this from the first time you eat or suck your thumb as a baby. Most of the microbes that get into the mouth die, but some survive.

Most plaque forms where the teeth meet the gums and in the gaps between the teeth (right). The photo below shows a tooth with a cavity.

WHAT ARE BACTERIA?

Bacteria are the tiniest living things. Each bacterium is a single living **cell,** but they usually grow together in colonies of billions, often many different kinds together.

The cells in animals and plants have many different structures inside them, in particular a large **nucleus.** Bacterial cells, however, are smaller and have no nucleus.

At birth your body contains no **bacteria,** but it begins to pick them up almost right away. The saliva (spit) in your mouth contains **antibiotics** that kill some microbes. Those that are swallowed are killed by the strong **acid** in your stomach. But some microbes, mostly bacteria, survive and begin to grow.

Tooth microbes

Most of the microbes in the mouth live on the teeth. Large numbers of bacteria build up in these areas. They form a sticky coating called **plaque,** which is made up of bacteria, saliva, and bits of food.

Plaque is only a thin film on the teeth, but it contains millions of bacteria. The most common ones are two types of *Streptococcus.* Both of these produce acid as a waste product. The acid can cause tooth decay because it gradually wears away the hard **enamel** on the teeth. Regular brushing helps to stop the buildup of plaque and can prevent tooth decay.

Although too much plaque is a bad thing, it would not be good to remove all the microbes from the mouth. Harmless mouth microbes use up the space and food that might otherwise be taken up by disease-causing microbes. In fact, our normal mouth bacteria also produce chemicals that kill other bacteria. They do this for their own benefit, but it helps our body's defenses, too.

This photo shows plaque (yellow) on the surface of a tooth magnified 200 times.

Bacteria in the Gut

Microbes that are swallowed with food are killed by strong **acids** in the stomach. Because of this, the **small intestine,** where most **digestion** takes place, has very few microbes. But more **bacteria** live in the **large intestine** than in any other part of the body.

The food that reaches the large intestine contains material that our bodies cannot use. But some bacteria can use our wastes as food, so they grow well in there.

The gut is like a long tube through the body. Food is mixed and digestion begins in the stomach (top, red). Most digestion takes place in the small intestine (blue), and wastes pass out through the large intestine, or bowel (orange).

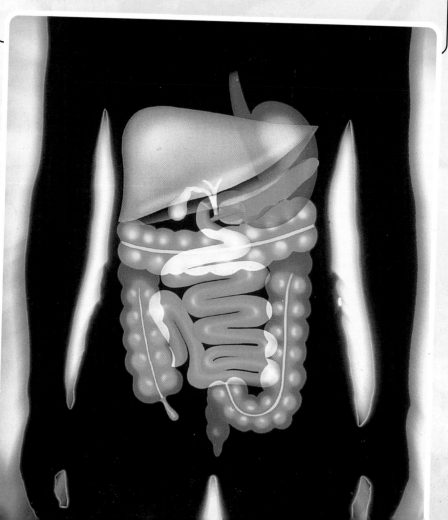

Chemical wizards

One of the main substances in plants is cellulose, a tough material that forms part of plant **cell** walls. Humans cannot break down cellulose, so it passes into the large intestine and out of the body. But many bacteria are chemical wizards and can make use of foods that we cannot. Some bacteria can break down cellulose and many other human wastes.

Many of the bacteria in your large intestine are **anaerobic.** This means that they do not need oxygen to live. When anaerobic microbes break down food for energy, the waste products are acids, alcohol, or a type of gas called methane. Too many

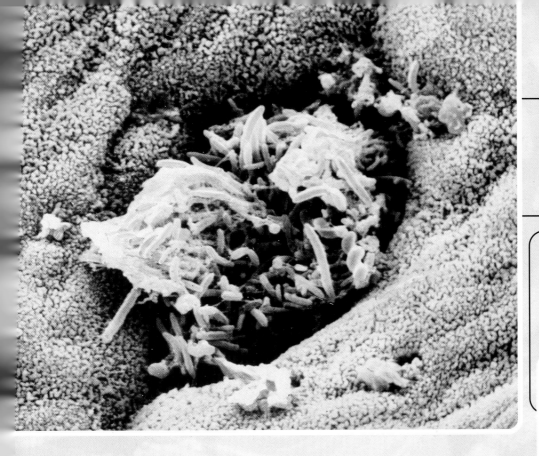

This cluster of Escherichia coli bacteria has settled on the wall of someone's large intestine (x4942).

Bacteroides (x19,585) is one of the anaerobic bacteria found in the large intestine.

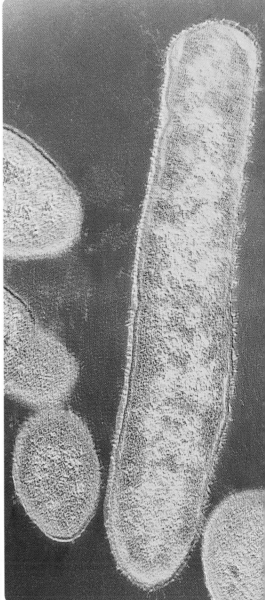

methane-producing bacteria in our large intestine can cause gas, or **flatulence.**

Helpful bacteria

Like the bacteria in the mouth, those in the large intestine do not harm us. Some **gut** bacteria are even helpful. One group produces vitamin K, which helps the blood **clot.** The bacteria make vitamin K for their own use, but when they die our body can absorb their vitamin K. Other bacteria in the gut produce B vitamins. This group of vitamins helps us get energy from food, makes sure our nerves work properly, and is important for healthy skin, hair, eyes, and liver.

OUTNUMBERED BY MICROBES

Our bodies are made up of billions of cells, but there even more bacteria in our large intestine. About 100,000 billion microbes live there, 10 times the number of cells in our bodies. Many microbes are passed out of the body in the **feces,** or bowel movements. Bacteria make up 25 to 50 percent of the dry weight of feces.

Trouble in the Gut

Sometimes **bacteria** that do not belong in the gut get in there and cause illness. They may cause food poisoning, **ulcers,** and other diseases.

Food poisoning

Although stomach **acid** kills most bacteria, a few types are tough enough to survive. These bacteria get through the stomach because they are eaten with foods such as stale milk or meat, which reduce the strength of the stomach acid. One example is *Salmonella,* which causes food poisoning. Once they have got past the stomach, *Salmonella* bacteria invade the lining of the intestine. They produce toxins, or poisons, that cause **diarrhea** and vomiting.

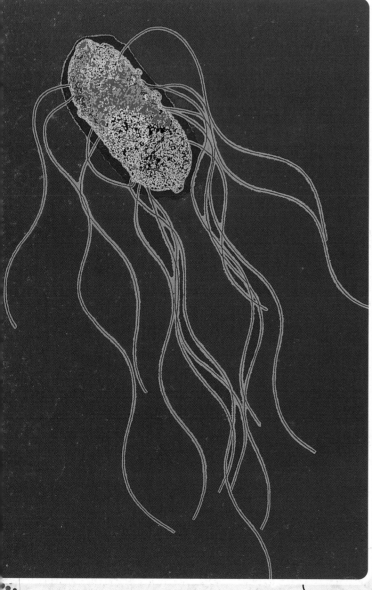

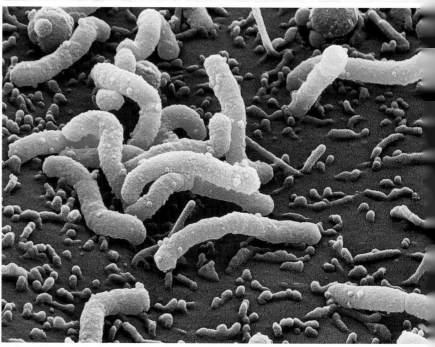

These Helicobacter *bacteria are on the surface of a human stomach* **cell.**

Salmonella *bacteria can grow in large numbers on food left out in warm conditions.*

Many other bacteria also cause food poisoning. Some, such as *Campylobacter,* normally live on the skin, but they cause illness if large numbers get into the **gut.** With other bacteria, such as *Escherichia coli,* there are certain specific types that can cause disease.

Ulcers

Another kind of bacterium, called *Helicobacter,* does not just survive the stomach. It lives there! *Helicobacter* is a fragile, spiral bacterium (*helico* means "spiral"). So how does it live in the harsh environment of the stomach?

The stomach lining has a thick coating of **mucus** to protect the stomach walls from acid. *Helicobacter* survives by getting through this mucus coating and fastening itself to the stomach wall. The mucus that protects the stomach wall also protects the bacteria.

Many people have *Helicobacter* in their stomachs. More than half the people over the age of 50 are infected. In some people it causes little harm. However, *Helicobacter* produces toxins that damage the stomach. In some people these toxins can cause stomach diseases such as ulcers and stomach cancer.

Microbes in the water

Cholera is a disease caused by a bacterium called *Vibrio cholerae.* It is rare in Europe and North America but common in places such as India and parts of Africa. A person may get cholera by drinking **contaminated** water. The symptoms are diarrhea, vomiting, and leg cramps. Although cholera can be life-threatening, it is easily prevented and treated.

John Snow was a doctor in London in the 1800s. He was the first doctor to recognize that cholera on by contaminated water.

Worms!

Do you have a dog or cat that has had worms? You might have had to take your pet to the vet to get rid of them. People can get worms, too, though this is much less common than in pets. **Tapeworms** and **hookworms** are just two of the many types of worms that are **parasites** of humans.

Tapeworms and hookworms are not related to each other, or to earthworms. Both live in the gut, but they get there by different routes and eat different foods.

Hookworms

Hookworms are the kind of worms your dog or cat is most likely to get. Some types can infect humans, but this does not often happen in **developed countries** because they have better **sanitation** than in poorer countries.

A severe infection with hookworms can create serious health problems for newborn babies, children, pregnant women, and people who have a poor diet.

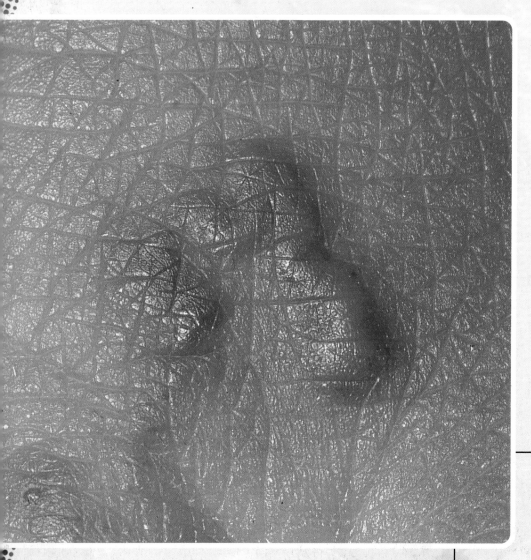

*If a hookworm **larva** gets into the body but cannot find a blood vessel, it causes a nasty rash.*

Getting into humans

Hookworm eggs begin life in the soil, where they hatch and grow into young worms. The young worms stand on their tails and wave their bodies in the air, searching for a passing human. They most often get into the body by making a hole in the skin of someone walking barefoot. The tiny young hookworms wriggle into a blood vessel and travel in the blood to the lungs, where they grow and develop further.

Becoming adults

When they are almost mature, the young hookworms are coughed out of the lungs and enter the **digestive** tract. They attach themselves to the wall of the intestine, where they live by sucking the **host's** blood. Soon they start to lay eggs, which pass out in the host's **feces.** In some countries, untreated **sewage** is released into rivers, and the river water is used for **irrigation.** If this happens, the eggs get into the soil, and the cycle begins again.

Effects of hookworms

When hookworms first get into the body, the place where they enter is itchy. Once they get into the **gut,** they may make a grown-up feel a bit ill. But children, and adults who do not get enough food, can become very ill from hookworms. Medicine will get rid of hookworms, but it is important to improve the diet to become completely healthy again.

A hookworm (x495) uses its mouthparts to cling to its host's intestines.

Tapeworms

Hookworms are only about 0.4 inch (1 cm) long. **Tapeworms** are 0.1 inch (3 mm) wide, but they can be more than 30 feet (10 m) long. These giant **parasites** live in humans only as adults. Their young live in another **host** animal. The pork tapeworm, for instance, spends its early life inside a pig.

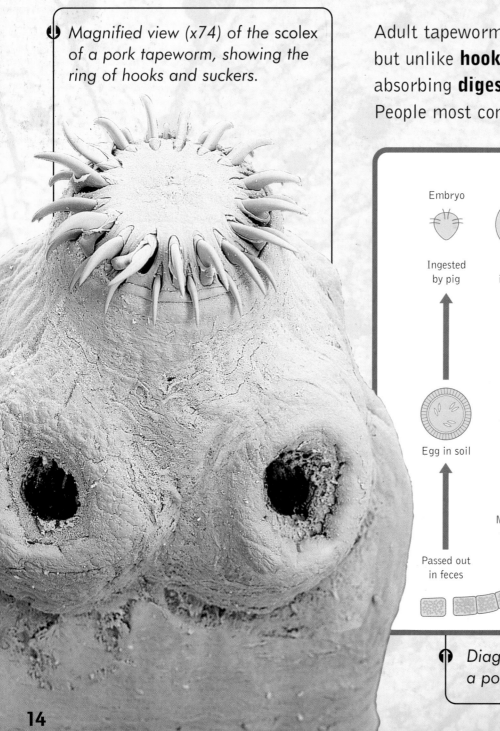

Magnified view (x74) of the scolex of a pork tapeworm, showing the ring of hooks and suckers.

Adult tapeworms live in human intestines, but unlike **hookworms,** they eat by absorbing **digested** food from the intestine. People most commonly get tapeworms by

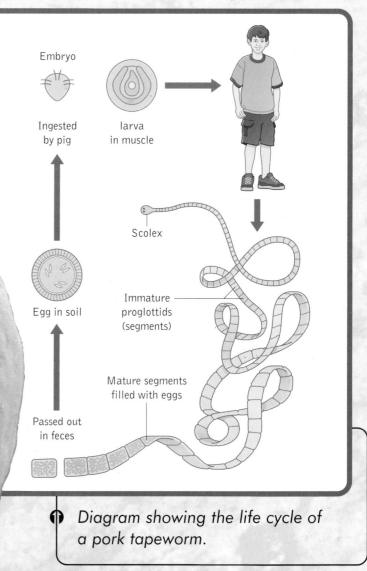

Embryo

Ingested by pig

larva in muscle

Scolex

Egg in soil

Immature proglottids (segments)

Mature segments filled with eggs

Passed out in feces

Diagram showing the life cycle of a pork tapeworm.

eating **contaminated** food that has not been cooked properly. (When food is thoroughly heated during cooking, any **microbes** in it are killed off.) However, food safety laws have almost completely gotten rid of tapeworms in **developed countries.**

The pork tapeworm

The pork tapeworm fastens to the wall of the human host's intestines using a ring of hooks and suckers, called a **scolex,** on its head. It then grows a long string of segments (up to 4,000 of them), each one containing thousands of eggs. When a segment is mature, it drops off the end of the worm and passes out in the host's **feces.** A large tapeworm can shed up to a million eggs a day.

Tapeworm eggs hatch into **larvae.** The larvae need to be eaten by a pig to grow further. This can happen if, for instance, pigs are fed plants that have been grown with water that is **contaminated** by untreated

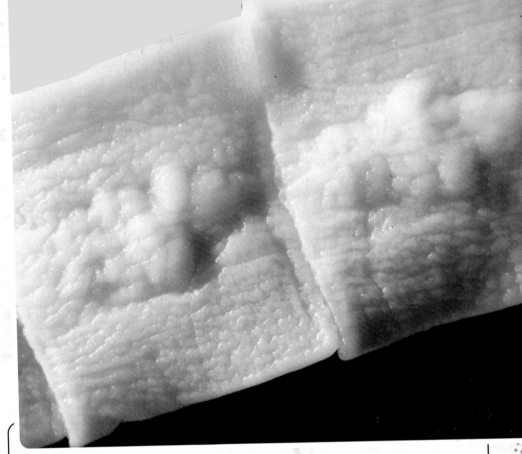

The fish tapeworm is the longest kind found in humans. It can live for twenty years. Here you can see a close-up of the tapeworm sections bulging with developing eggs.

human **sewage.** Once the larvae are eaten, they get into the pig's blood and travel to the muscles. There each one forms a tough ball called a **cyst.**

If the pig is killed for meat, the cysts get into another human. Once it has reached the human intestine, the cyst splits and turns itself inside out to become the head of a new adult tapeworm. The cycle is ready to begin again.

Tapeworm symptoms

As with hookworms, a healthy adult can be infected with a tapeworm and have only mild discomfort for a time. However, a bad tapeworm infection can cause **diarrhea** and vomiting. Some people are constantly hungry because the tapeworms are eating most of their food. Drugs can get rid of the worm.

Microbes in the Nose and Throat

When you breathe in, tiny particles of dust get into your nose and throat along with the air. Some of this dust is **microbes** such as **bacteria** and **viruses.** Scientists estimate that we inhale 10,000 new microbes every day.

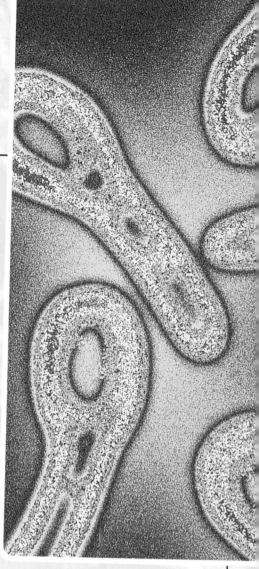

Corynebacterium *can be club-shaped, as shown here (x100,000). Some kinds can cause the serious disease called diphtheria.*

Many of the microbes that we inhale are trapped and killed by the body's defenses. However, some survive and live in the nose and throat.

Bacteria

Two main groups of bacteria live in the nose and throat. One group is made up of

This photo shows Staphylococcus *bacteria (round, yellow shapes) on the lining of the nose (x17,160). The nose is lined with tiny hairs called* **cilia.** *The bacteria cling to the* **mucus** *(blue) on the cilia.*

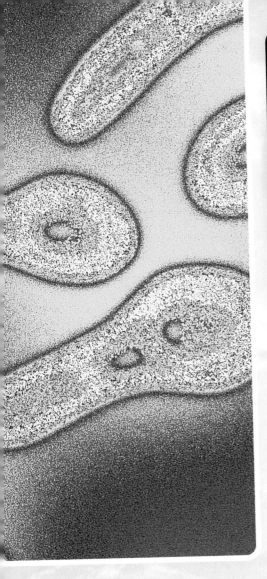

VIRUSES

Viruses are tiny particles made of an outer layer that is mainly protein and an inner core of **DNA.**

Outside of another living cell, a virus cannot move, eat, grow, or reproduce. Viruses infect cells by injecting their into the cell. Then the virus takes control. It puts the cell's machinery to work making copies of the virus. Eventually the cell becomes overloaded and bursts, releasing thousands of viruses to infect other cells.

Corynebacterium. These bacteria are sausage-shaped rather than round.

Smaller than bacteria

Also living in the nose and throat are even smaller microbes called viruses. Some viruses live in the nose and throat even in healthy people. Viruses differ from other creatures because they can grow and reproduce only when they are inside the **cells** of another living thing (see box).

There are all kinds of different viruses in the nose and throat. Adenoviruses live mainly on the tonsils, while myxoviruses live in the tissues of the nose and throat. Rhinoviruses are

small, round bacteria called *Staphylococcus* (a coccus is any kind of round or oval-shaped bacterium). They grow in chains, or in clusters like bunches of grapes. Some kinds of *Staphylococcus* can cause illness, but others live in the nose and throat without causing any harm.

The other bacteria common in the nose and throat are members of a group called

Adenoviruses are not round. They look like crystals, with 20 flat, triangular-shaped faces (x167,650).

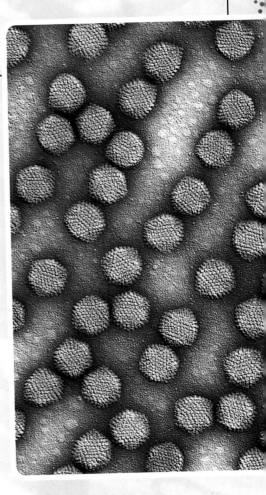

very tiny viruses that also live in the nose and throat.

Sore Throats, Colds, and the Flu

Aaaaa-choo! Sneezes, coughing, and a runny nose usually mean a cold or flu. Colds and flu are caused when the **viruses** in your nose and throat get past the defenses that normally keep them in check. **Bacteria** can also cause illnesses such as sore throats.

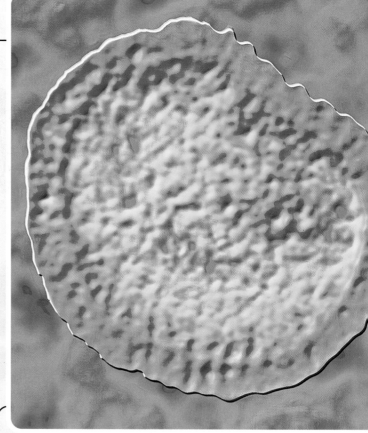

The hairlike **cilia** (pink) that line the throat clear out most of the **microbes** before they can take hold (x1970).

This is the influenza virus (x462,185), which causes flu. Other viruses in the nose cause different illness.

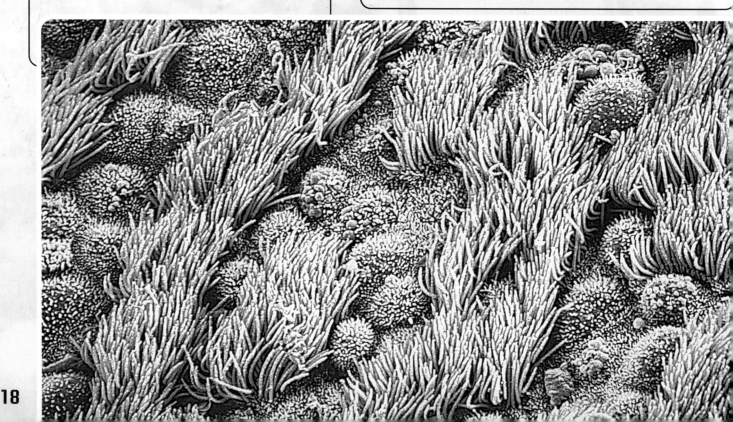

18

Getting a cold

Colds are caused by tiny viruses called rhinoviruses. There are many different kinds of rhinoviruses, and each kind can sometimes **mutate**, which fools your body's defenses.

If a rhinovirus manages to get into one of the **cells** that line the nose, it takes over and makes copies of itself. Eventually the cell bursts open and releases many new viruses, which invade more cells.

Though cold viruses damage the nose lining, they do not cause cold symptoms. The symptoms mainly result from the body's response to the infection. The body releases chemicals that increase the flow of **mucus** in the nose and cause sneezing and coughing. The combination of sneezing, coughing, and a runny nose helps to clear viruses out of the nose and throat.

Bacterial infections

Bacteria can also cause sore throats or tonsillitis (see box). A bacterium that causes sore throats is called *Streptococcus,* so this kind of sore throat is called strep throat. Strep throat can cause a lot of pain, but doctors can treat it with **antibiotics**.

TONSILLITIS

The tonsils are two pink balls in the back of the throat. You can see them if you stand in front of a mirror, open your mouth, stick out your tongue and say, "Aaahh."

The job of the tonsils is to catch microbes. Sometimes the tonsils themselves get infected, and the result is tonsillitis. Usually gargling, taking painkillers, and keeping the throat cool will get rid of the infection. But sometimes **antibiotics** are needed, and some people get tonsillitis so often that they have to have their tonsils removed.

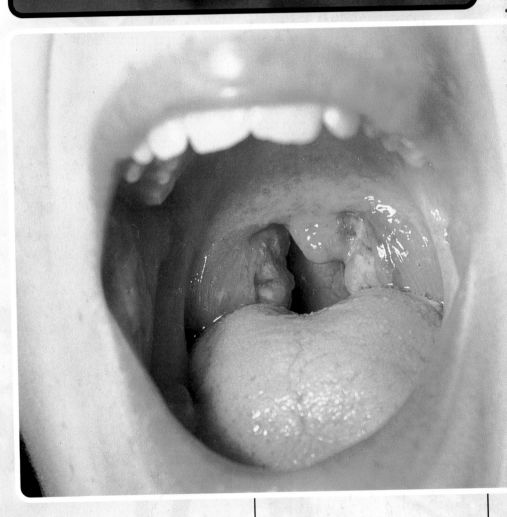

These tonsils are swollen by infection with Streptococcus.

However, these drugs do not work for sore throats caused by viruses.

Microbes in the lungs

When a healthy person breathes, **microbes** do not get any farther into the body than the throat. But sometimes microbes do get into the lungs and cause diseases.

Any microbes that get beyond the throat are usually trapped in a thick layer of **mucus** that covers the walls of the tubes. They are then pushed out of the lungs by millions of tiny hairlike **cells** called **cilia,** which wave the microbes up into the throat. The microbes are then swallowed and killed by the **acids** in the stomach.

Getting into the lungs

Some microbes can, however, get past this first line of defense. They have special chemicals on the outside that allow them to fasten on to the lung lining. Then other chemicals called **invasins** help them get into the body.

Pneumonia

One disease caused by lung infection is pneumonia. Pneumonia is a serious infection in which some of the air sacs in the lungs become inflamed, or swollen.

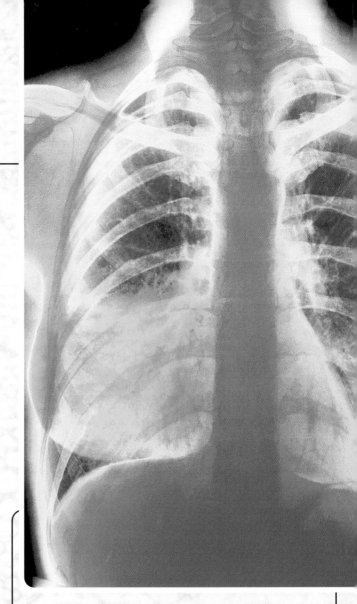

This is an X ray of the lungs of someone with pneumonia. In the affected area (light blue), the air sacs get blocked with pus, causing the lung to get hard.

This causes breathlessness, a chesty cough, fever, chills, and chest pain.

Pneumonia can have several different causes. One type is caused by *Streptococcus* **bacteria,** similar to the ones that cause strep throat. Several different **viruses** can also cause other types of pneumonia, although they are not as serious.

Another mild type of pneumonia is caused by **mycoplasmas,** which are very, very small, unusual bacteria. All other bacteria have a tough outer wall, but mycoplasmas have only a thin, bendable membrane, or skin.

Whooping cough and TB

Two other lung diseases are whooping cough and tuberculosis (TB). Both are spread by the coughs and sneezes of infected people, which spray tiny droplets containing the bacteria into the air.

Whooping cough is caused by a bacterium called *Bordetella.* In the past it was a serious disease, but now there is a **vaccine** against it.

TB is caused by the bacterium *Mycobacterium tuberculosis.* It usually starts as a lung disease, but it can spread to other parts of the body. The disease causes fever, weight loss, and constant coughing. Drugs have been developed against TB, but the disease is still a problem in poor countries, where there is not enough money for good health care and drugs.

Mycobacterium tuberculosis *is the bacterium that causes tuberculosis (x25,035).*

Babies in many countries are given a single vaccination that protects them against three diseases—whooping cough, diphtheria, and tetanus.

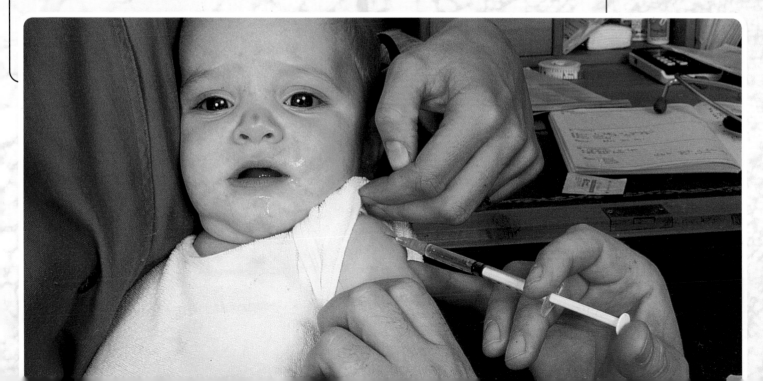

Microbes in the Blood

Your skin seems quite thin and not very tough, but it keeps all kinds of **microbes** out of the body. However, sometimes the skin is broken by a cut or a scrape.

Wound defenses

If you get a cut or a scrape, the body's defense systems go into action. The blood at the site of the wound **clots,** or gets hard, and the clot blocks microbes. Also, many **white blood cells** rush to the site of the wound. Some of these blood cells can eat microbes. Other white blood cells break open and release chemicals that kill microbes.

Ouch! If you get a cut or a scrape, it hurts! But your body's defense system quickly starts repairing it.

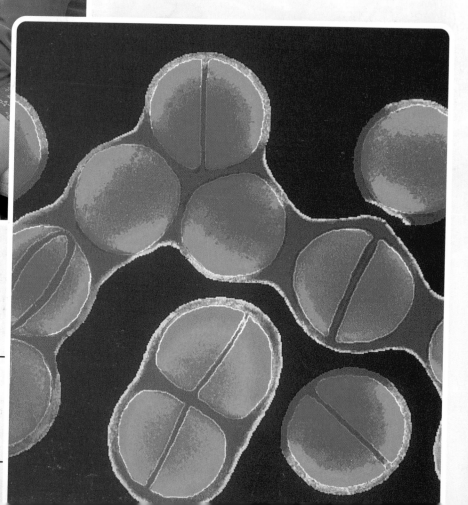

Staphylococcus bacteria like these (x26,890) can cause a cut to become infected.

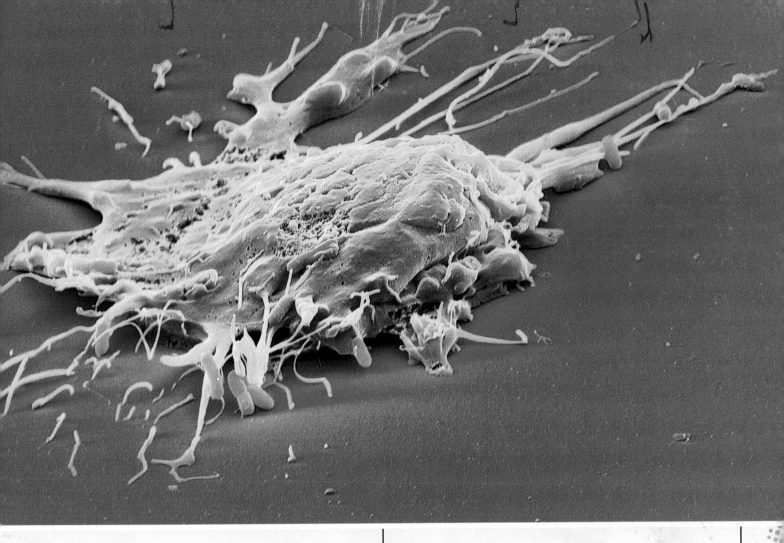

Septic cuts

If you clean a wound carefully and then cover it with a bandage, the body can usually heal itself. However, a deep wound (for instance from a nail) might be difficult to clean and may get infected. If this happens, the area around the cut may get red and begin to swell as more and more white blood cells arrive to combat the infection. The wound may also produce a yellow discharge called pus, which is made up of dead microbes and the remains of white blood cells.

If **bacteria** or other microbes get out of the local area of the wound and into the blood, they can travel in the bloodstream and cause infection elsewhere.

This white blood cell is reaching out long feelers to take in several bacteria (pink, rod-shaped) (x5882). Once inside the blood cell, the bacteria are broken down.

Infection microbes

The microbes that usually get into a wound are ones that are normally found on the skin, such as some kinds of *Staphylococcus.* However, sometimes bacteria from soil or other places get into a wound and cause illness. Tetanus, for instance, is a disease in which the muscles go into **spasm.** It is caused by a bacterium normally found in the soil. Tetanus used to be a serious danger, but in many countries people are now vaccinated against the disease.

Diseases from Bloodsuckers

Sometimes **microbes** get past the body's outer defenses by being injected directly into the blood. This can happen if you get bitten by a bloodsucking insect or other animal. Mosquitoes, ticks, and fleas are three bloodsuckers that can pass on disease this way.

Most of us have been bitten by mosquitoes, midges, or other bloodsuckers. Most of the time the bite causes nothing more than an itchy lump. But the insect that bites you might be carrying microbes that cause disease, and these microbes get into your blood.

A mosquito feeds on a human. Only female mosquitoes are bloodsuckers. Male mosquitoes drink nectar from flowers.

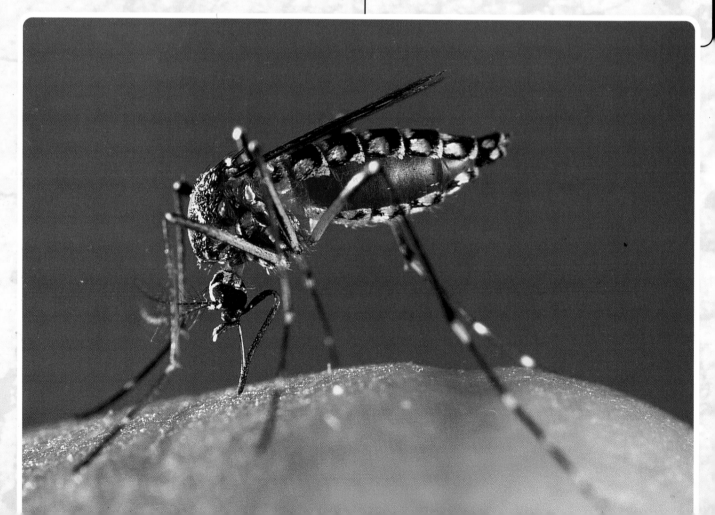

Insect-carried diseases are a particular problem in tropical countries.

When a bloodsucker bites a person, it injects saliva (spit) into the wound. Chemicals in the saliva stop the blood from **clotting.** If the bloodsucker is carrying a disease, microbes get into the blood with the saliva.

Mosquitoes

Mosquitoes are carriers of more diseases than any other bloodsuckers. They can carry malaria, a disease that causes many human deaths every year (see page 26). They can also carry other diseases. The West Nile **virus** is carried by mosquitoes and causes a flulike fever. But it can have more severe effects, such as causing the brain to swell.

Ticks

Ticks are eight-legged bloodsuckers that are relatives of spiders. One illness that can be passed on in tick bites is Lyme disease. It is caused by a spiral-shaped **bacterium**

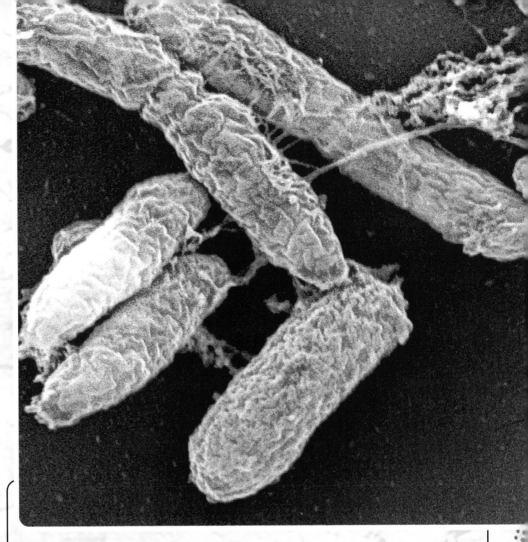

Yersinia pestis *bacteria cause plague.*

called *Borrelia.* Lyme disease starts with a rash around the site of the tick bite but then causes painful swelling of joints called arthritis.

Fleas

The fleas that sometimes infest our pets and that occasionally bite us usually do not carry diseases. But they can pass **tapeworms** on to dogs and cats if they accidentally swallow them (see page 14). Fleas also can

carry several other unpleasant diseases.

The bacteria that cause plague, *Yersinia pestis,* are carried by rat fleas. Plague makes people feverish and exhausted, and they get painful swellings in their armpits and necks. Plague killed millions of people in Asia and Europe in the 1300s, and there are still regular outbreaks in Africa, Asia, and South America.

Protozoans

Bacteria and **viruses** are not the only **microbes** that live inside us. Larger single-celled creatures called **protozoans** also live there. Some are **parasites** and cause disease, but others are **predators** that feed on other microbes.

These amoebas (blue) are attached to and feeding on the lining of the large intestine (x3177).

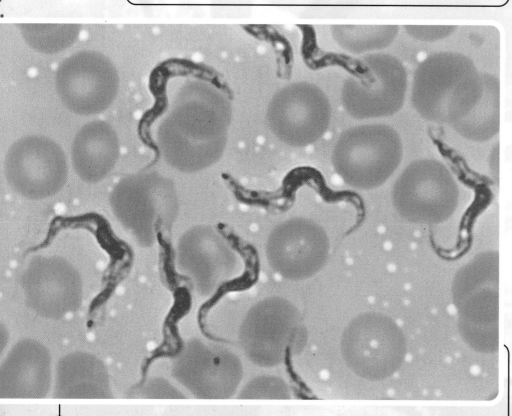

A magnified view (x2550) of the blood of someone with sleeping sickness shows the Trypansoma flagellates that cause the disease (blue) among the red blood cells (gray, round).

Amoebas

Amoebas are protozoans that live in the mouth and parts of the **gut.** They get into the mouth with food or from our fingers and feed on **bacteria** and small bits of food.

An amoeba is a jellylike blob with a thin, bendable membrane, or skin. It moves by sending out long, fingerlike **pseudopods** that attach to a surface then pull the amoeba forward. Amoebas also use their pseudopods to catch food.

water that has been **contaminated** by **sewage.** *Giardia* infections often cause diarrhea.

Other flagellates live in the blood and are spread by bloodsucking insects. One kind causes sleeping sickness, a serious disease in tropical Africa that is spread by a fly.

Malaria

Malaria is one of the most serious diseases in humans. In the hot regions of Africa, southern Asia, and South America, millions of people get the disease each year, and many of them die. Malaria is caused by a type of protozoan called *Plasmodium.* It begins its life in a mosquito and gets into people's blood when the mosquito bites them. The protozoans mostly infect red blood **cells.** They multiply until the blood cell bursts, and then they invade another cell. If another mosquito feeds on a person infected with malaria, it might pick up protozoans from the blood. Then the disease cycle starts all over again.

One kind of amoeba that can get into the gut feeds on the wall of the stomach or intestines instead of feeding on bacteria. This kind of amoeba can cause bad **diarrhea.**

Other protozoans

Other kinds of protozoans can also get into the gut and cause disease. A tiny, slipper-shaped protozoan called *Giardia* belongs to a group of protozoans called **flagellates.** It can infect the **small intestine** if people eat food or drink

⚑ *Plasmodium protozoans (yellow) break out from red blood cells (x10,040).*

Table of Sizes

Although all hidden life is tiny, there is a huge range of sizes. To a flea, a white blood cell seems just as tiny as the flea seems to us.

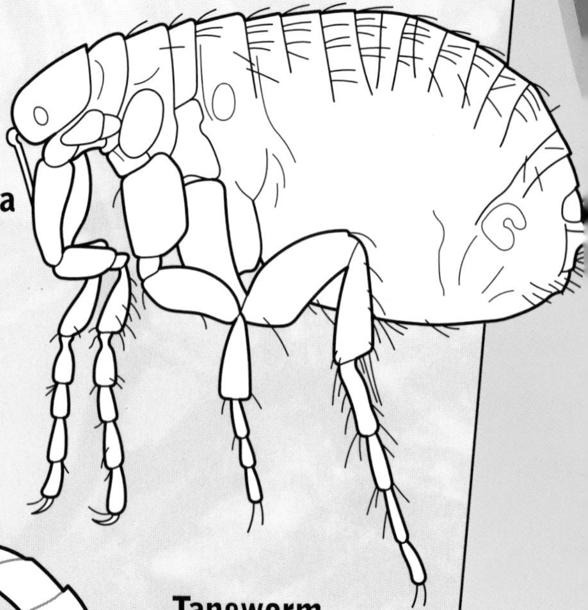

Rat flea
4 mm

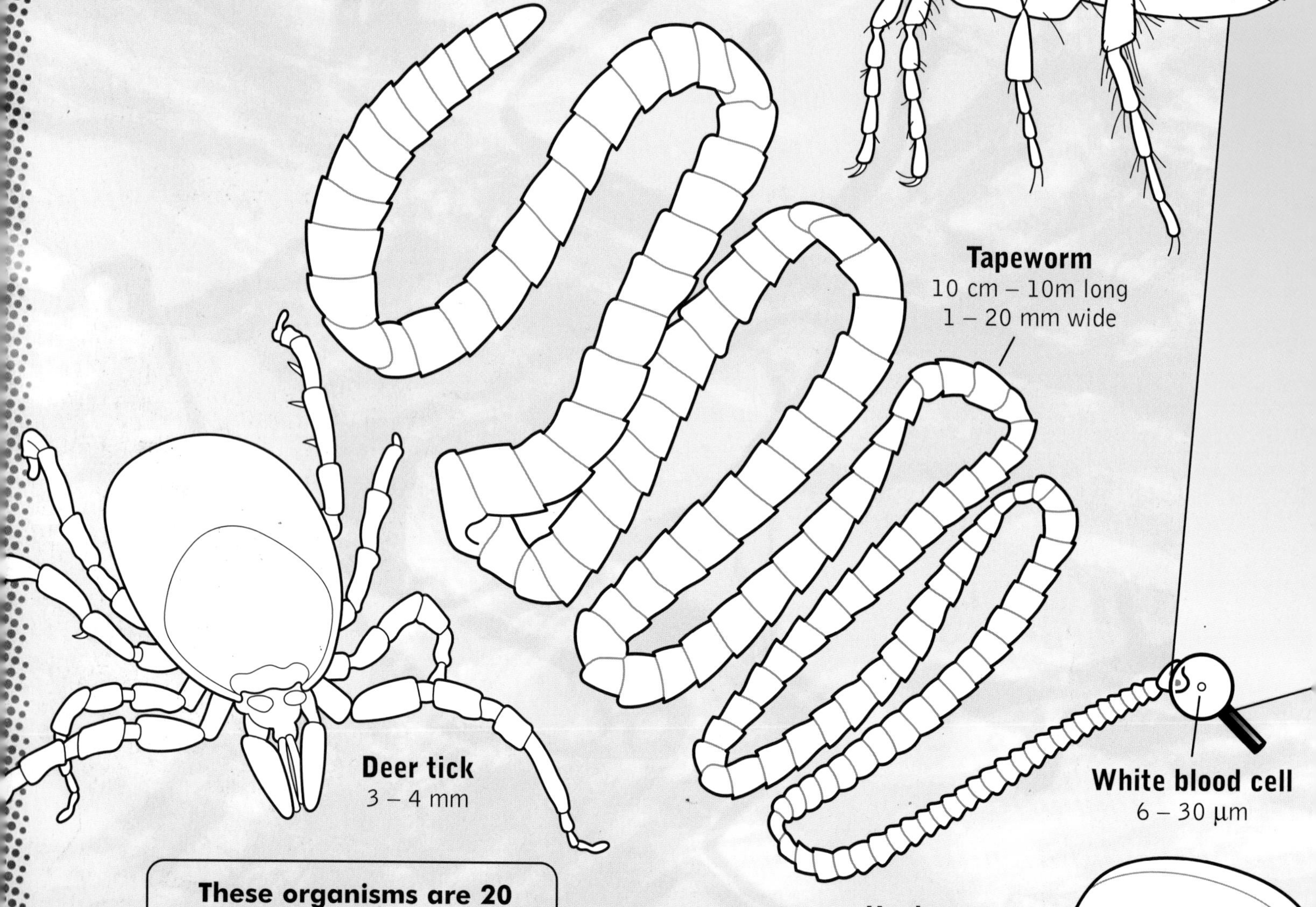

Tapeworm
10 cm – 10m long
1 – 20 mm wide

Deer tick
3 – 4 mm

White blood cell
6 – 30 µm

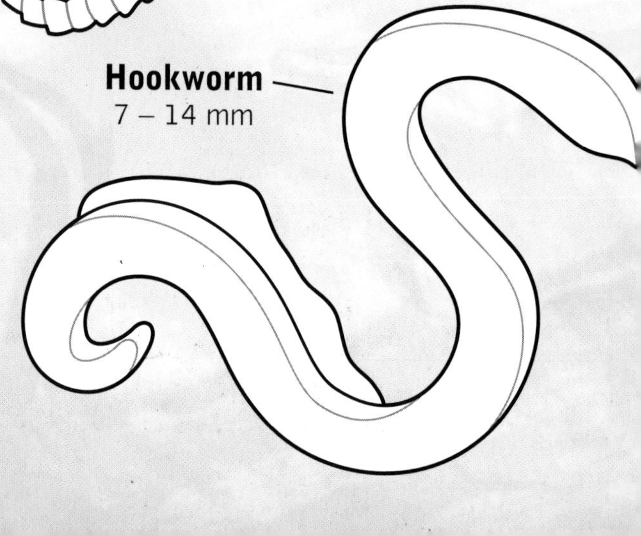

Hookworm
7 – 14 mm

These organisms are 20 times bigger than normal.

HOW SMALL?

1 m (meter) = 1,000 mm (millimeters)
1 mm (millimeter) = 1,000 µm (micrometers)
1 µm (micrometer) = 1,000 nm (nanometers)

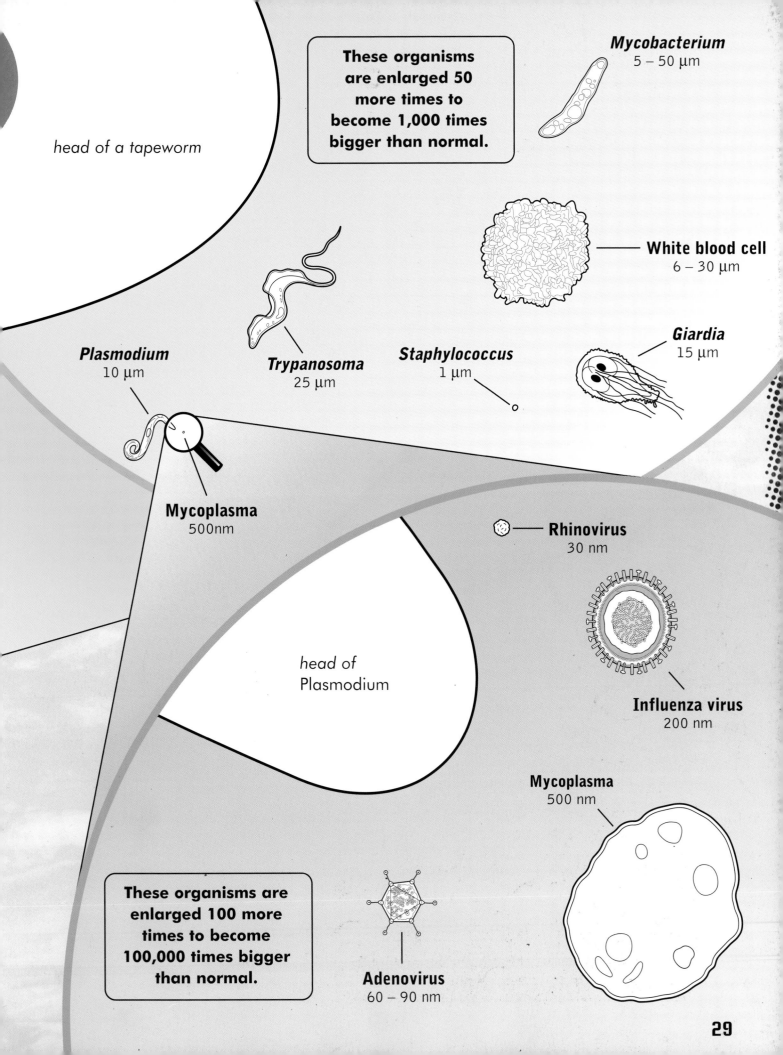

head of a tapeworm

These organisms are enlarged 50 more times to become 1,000 times bigger than normal.

Mycobacterium
5 – 50 μm

White blood cell
6 – 30 μm

Trypanosoma
25 μm

Staphylococcus
1 μm

Giardia
15 μm

Plasmodium
10 μm

Mycoplasma
500nm

Rhinovirus
30 nm

head of
Plasmodium

Influenza virus
200 nm

Mycoplasma
500 nm

These organisms are enlarged 100 more times to become 100,000 times bigger than normal.

Adenovirus
60 – 90 nm

Glossary

acid   substance that is sour, sharp, or able to dissolve other substances. Lemon juice and vinegar are acids.

anaerobic   without air. Anaerobic microbes can live without air.

antibiotic   drug or natural chemical that kills bacteria or stops them from growing

bacteria   microscopic living things, each one only a single cell. They are different from other one-celled creatures because they do not have a nucleus. Only one of these living things is called a bacterium.

cells   building blocks of living things. Some living things are single cells, while others are made up of billions of cells working together.

cilia   tiny hairlike structures that stick out from the surface of some microbes. They can beat together in a rhythm to move the microbe along or wave food toward it. Only one of these structures is called a cilium.

clot   lump of hardened blood

contaminated   when food or something else becomes dirty or infected with disease microbes

cyst   round capsule with a tough outer coat. Pork hookworms form cysts in the muscles of pigs.

developed countries   countries such as those of Europe and North America, where most people work in offices and factories rather than as farmers

diarrhea   watery bowel movement

digestion   breaking down of the food we eat into nutrients that the body can absorb and use for energy

DNA   material that makes up the genes of living cells

electron microscope   very powerful microscope that can magnify objects up to 500,000 times

enamel   hard protective coating on the outside of teeth

feces   solid waste from the digestive system

flagellate   a type of protozoan that has one or more long, whiplike hairs called flagella

flatulence   trapped gas in the gut causing discomfort

gut   digestive tract, which includes the stomach and intestines

hookworms   small worms that are parasites of humans and other animals

host   animal or plant that a parasite lives on

invasins   chemicals produced by disease microbes that help them to invade the body

irrigation   to water fields of crops

large intestine   the last part of the gut, where water is absorbed from waste food and the waste becomes feces

larva   the young stage of some types of insects. A larva looks different from an adult and has to go through a changing stage (the pupa) in order to become an adult.

microbe   microscopic creature such as a bacterium, protozoan, fungus, or virus

mucus   thick, gooey liquid that helps to protect the lining of the air tubes and the gut

mutate   to change shape or form

mycoplasma   very small bacterium that does not have a hard outer cell wall

nucleus   round structure surrounded by a membrane, found inside a living cell. It contains the cell's genes.

parasite   creature that lives on or in another living creature and takes its food from it, without giving any benefit in return and sometimes causing harm

plaque   thin film of bacteria that covers parts of the teeth

predator   animal that hunts and kills other animals for food

proteins   substances that are used to build structures within living things and to control the thousands of chemical reactions that happen inside cells

protozoan   single-celled creature that has larger, more complicated cells than bacteria

pseudopod   fingerlike structure that an amoeba sends out in order to move around and to capture food. The word means "false foot."

sanitation   keeping houses and streets clean, making sure that food is safe to eat, and disposing of waste safely

scolex   head of a tapeworm, including a circle of hooks and suckers, which it uses to attach to the intestines

sewage   waste from sinks, bathrooms, and toilets

small intestine   main part of the gut, a long tube between the stomach and the large intestine where the body absorbs most of the nutrients from our food

spasm sudden, uncontrollable contraction, or shortening, of a muscle

tapeworm long flatworm made up of many segments that is a parasite of humans and other animals

ulcer sore on the lining of the stomach or intestines

vaccine substance that protects a person from getting a certain disease by starting up the body's defenses against that disease

virus an extremely tiny microbe that cannot grow or reproduce by itself, but has to infect a living cell to do so

white blood cell cell in the blood that plays an important part in defending the body against disease

More Books to Read

Bailey, Jill. *Life in the Human Body.* Chicago: Raintree Publishers, 2003.

Barnes, Kate. *Inside the Human Body.* Milwaukee, Wisc.: Gareth Stevens, 2001.

Branzei, Sylvia. *Hands-On Grossology.* New York: Price Stern Sloan, 2003.

Hirschmann, Kris. *Salmonella.* Farmington Hills, Mich.: Gale Group, 2004.

Jarrow, Gail. *Hookworms.* Farmington Hills, Mich.: Gale Group, 2004.

Viegas, Jennifer. *Parasites.* New York: Rosen Publishing, 2003.

Ward, Brian R. *Microscopic Life in Your Body.* North Mankato, Minn.: Smart Apple Media, 2004.

Index